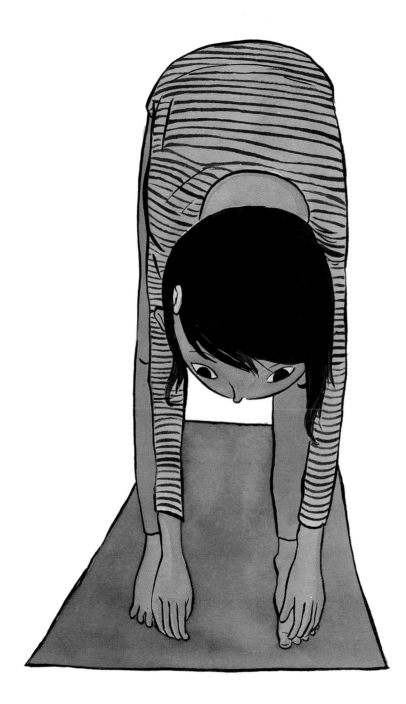

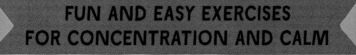
FUN AND EASY EXERCISES
FOR CONCENTRATION AND CALM

ANY
TIME
YOGA

ULRIKA DEZÉ

ILLUSTRATIONS BY SIMON KROUG

bala kids

BOULDER

The author and illustrator would like to thank Anne Terral.

Bala Kids
An imprint of Shambhala Publications, Inc.
4720 Walnut Street
Boulder, Colorado 80301
shambhala.com

Translation © 2019 Shambhala Publications, Inc.
Originally published as *Le Yoga de Kika* by Éditions MILAN ©
2011 Ulrika Dezé and Simon Kroug

This book in not intended to diagnose, treat, cure, or prevent
any disease. The exercises are meant to be practiced
with children with adult supervision and may need to be
modified for any child's particular physical condition.

yogaminiparis.com

9 8 7 6 5 4 3 2 1

First U.S. Edition
Printed in China

♾ This edition is printed on acid-free paper that meets the
American National Standards Institute Z39.48 Standard.

♻ Shambhala Publications makes every effort to print
on recycled paper. For more information please visit
www.shambhala.com.

Bala Kids is distributed worldwide by Penguin Random
House, Inc., and its subsidiaries.

Designed by Debbie Berne

Library of Congress Cataloging-in-Publication Data
Names: Dezé, Ulrika, author. | Kroug, Simon, illustrator.
Title: Anytime yoga: fun and easy exercises for
    concentration and calm / Ulrika Dezé; Illustrations
    by Simon Kroug.
Other titles: Yoga de Kika. English
Description: First U.S. edition. | Boulder, Colorado: Bala
    Kids, an imprint of Shambhala Publications, Inc., [2018]
    | Audience: Age 3–7. | "Originally published as Le Yoga de
    Kika by Éditions MILAN © 2011 Ulrika Dezé and Simon
    Kroug."
Identifiers: LCCN 2018047779 | ISBN 9781611804393
    (hardback: alk. paper)
Subjects: LCSH: Hatha yoga—Juvenile literature. |
    Relaxation—Juvenile literature.
Classification: LCC RA781.7 .D5213 2018 | DDC 613.7/046—
    dc23
LC record available at https://lccn.loc.gov/2018047779

May all kids everywhere awaken to
their own creativity and calm.

—ULRIKA DEZÉ

CONTENTS

INTRODUCTION

HELLO! My name is Kika. My little monkey Yazoo and I have just discovered something wonderful: YOGA.

Yoga is not complicated. It's like a game. You make movements with your arms, your legs—your whole body—imitating animals or things found in nature.

For example, sometimes you stand up tall like a tree and have to keep your balance. Sometimes you make little leaps like a frog. It is fun!

Since I started doing yoga, I feel stronger and more flexible. I breathe calmly. I can concentrate better, and I'm relaxed. Isn't that so, Yazoo?

Come along! You're invited to join me on a journey. We're going to learn fourteen yoga poses. You can do them by yourself or, of course, you can do them with the grown-ups in your life, your friends, or your teachers.

There are four chapters in this book. They are the four stages of our journey. The poses in the yellow chapter help us WAKE UP mindfully in the morning. The poses in the green chapter help us to CONCENTRATE. As we do the movements in the pink chapter we meet some interesting animals and become FULL OF ENERGY. Finally, the very gentle movements of the blue chapter help us CALM DOWN.

If you have fifteen minutes to an hour, you can enjoy following along with us on the whole journey. Or, if you only have a few minutes, you can pick out the chapter that goes best with the way you're feeling. At the end of each short session, read to yourself or ask somebody to read to you one of the guided meditations.

I love it when grown-ups read me the stories (beginning on page 38). I close my eyes, breathe deeply, relax all my muscles, and embark on a journey to a place that makes me dream, like a garden or under the water.

Quiet now, Yazoo! We're going to start soon!

BEFORE YOU BEGIN

- Wait a little while after eating, so you can stay light on your toes. (Isn't that right, Yazoo, my little banana muncher?)

- Pick a place in your house that is calm and cozy, a place where you feel comfortable but where you have enough room to move around.

- Make some space around yourself and ask an adult to turn off any noisy machines or devices that might disturb you.

- Take off your regular clothes and your shoes and pick out something comfortable to wear. I usually put on my sweatpants and my striped T-shirt.

- Use a small yoga mat to keep yourself from slipping. You unroll it on the floor, like I do on the next page.

- Put a small blanket and a pillow on the floor next to you. You'll need them when it is time to listen to the guided meditation.

- You can also put on some soft music if you feel like it.

- Breathe. Feel the air coming into your nostrils and listen to what your body tells you. Never force yourself!

OKAY! ARE YOU READY? LET'S GO!

XI

Good morning, sun!

It's morning, and you're there, shining brightly in the sky!

Thanks to your energy, we're going to be able to start our day off right.

This morning, we begin our journey.

GOOD MORNING POSE

Stand on your mat,

feet together,

back straight,

shoulders back,

palms of your hands joined at the level of your chest.

Look straight ahead into the distance,

and breathe calmly four times.

Before starting your yoga practice, it's a good idea to stretch from the tip of your toes to the top of your head!

I am strong and steady on my feet.

I am as tall as a mountain.

I can almost touch the sky!

MOUNTAIN POSE

Stand on your mat,

feet slightly apart,

back straight,

arms relaxed at your sides.

Clasping your hands together,

stretch your arms above your head

and tilt your head slightly back.

Then, with your hands still clasped,
come back to the starting point.

Repeat four times.

Tick tock, tick tock! Listen to this rhythmic sound.

Tick tock, tick tock! With that same kind of rhythm, you can sway back and forth like a swing rocking in the wind.

Breathe deeply! We are just about ready.

After this pose, go to page 38 and have someone read you "In the Sun."

6

PENDULUM POSE

Stand on your mat,

legs slightly apart,

and lean forward

to try to touch your toes.

Fully relax your face,

close your eyes,

breathe calmly,

and swing from left to right.

Repeat six times.

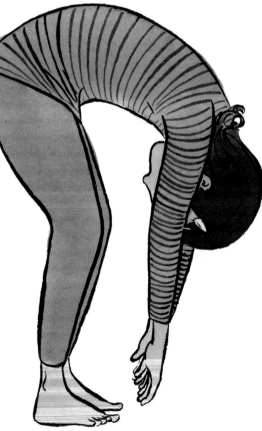

7

Spread your giant bird wings wide.

Swooping around among the clouds is fun!

It's so cool to fly!

AIRPLANE POSE

Stand on your mat,

legs slightly apart,

arms spread wide to the sides,

hands relaxed.

Balance carefully on your right foot,

then lean slightly forward

and gently stretch your left leg backward.

Breathe calmly.

Now balance on your left foot

and stretch your right leg back.

Repeat three times on each side.

That's it! We're here!

Look around! We're in a huge forest!

There are so many unfamiliar sounds
and smells and so many new colors.

Let's rest a little bit before we go
any further, okay?

CHILD'S POSE

Sit on your heels

and lean your upper body forward,

forehead to the floor,

arms relaxed and back along the sides of your body,

palms turned up toward the sky.

Close your eyes

and breathe calmly a few times.

Oh, wow! What's that?

It's a butterfly! It's beautiful!

It looks like somebody just finished painting its wings.

We can be light and beautiful too!

Come on, let's do some flying ourselves and follow it.

BUTTERFLY POSE

Sit on your mat,

back straight,

legs stretched out in front of you.

Bend your knees,

put the soles of your feet against
each other,

then raise and lower your knees gently
while firmly holding your feet with
your hands.

Repeat five or ten times while
breathing calmly.

How about landing on this tree? It's so tall! The leaves touch the clouds.

The roots are deep down in the earth.

It's a bit like an old grandfather of the forest, don't you think, Yazoo?

Let's imitate it!

After this pose, go to page 40 and have some read you "In the Garden."

16

TREE POSE

Stand on your mat,

back straight,

feet slightly apart and parallel,

and shoulders back.

Balance on your left foot,

then lift the right leg and place the sole of your right foot against your left thigh or calf.

If you wish, you can use the wall to help with balance.

Breathe in,

raise your arms above your head,

and join the palms of your hands together.

Breathe normally for three seconds.

Repeat three times on each side.

Whoa, do you see that!?
A lion! He's sitting
very still.

He shows us how proud
and strong he is and
gazes at us.

Oops! He gets angry and shows
his claws!

Now he opens his jaws wide—
look at those teeth!

But we're not a bit afraid!

And we roar right
along with him:
ROOOARRR!

LION POSE

Sit on your heels,

back straight.

Spread your knees slightly apart and rest your hands on them.

Take a deep breath in through your nose, taking in lots of air,

then open your mouth wide,

letting your tongue hang out

and say, "Haaa!"

Repeat four times.

Quick! Let's continue on with
our trip.

Say, Yazoo, could you teach me how
you leap from vine to vine?

We want to jump with you and
become kings of the jungle!

Hop! Hop! Hop!

MONKEY POSE

Stand on your mat,

lean your upper body forward

with your arms hanging down,

your legs slightly apart,

and your knees slightly bent.

Relax your head and
your arms

and do little jumps.

Repeat three times.

Shhh! A snake is showing her elegance and style!

It's a cobra!

She has finished her siesta in the sun.

To the sound of a flute, we ripple along with her.

And we let out a long hiss . . . SSSSSSSSS!

COBRA POSE

Lie down on your belly,

squeeze your legs together tight,

bend your elbows,

and put your palms on the floor near your shoulders

and your forehead on the floor.

Then take a big breath in,

push into your palms,

and raise your upper body,

leaning your head slightly back.

With your mouth slightly open,

breathe out

as you lower your upper body back to the floor,

letting out a long *SSSSSS!*

Repeat three times.

Look at that strange piece of wood in the water!

Wait: it's an enooormous crocodile!

His home is the river. He is super powerful!

Let's be as strong as he is!

After this pose, go to page 42 and have someone read you "In the Sky."

26

CROCODILE POSE

Lie down on your belly,

squeeze your legs together tight,

bend your elbows,

and put one hand on each cheek.

Look off into the distance straight ahead of you

with your eyes wide open and

breathe calmly four times.

I AM RESTING

Splash!

Something just jumped out of the water right there in front of us.

It sparkles, it wriggles, it spatters!

Let's plunge into the waves.

Let's be just like this shining, slippery fish!

FISH POSE

Lie on your back,

legs together,

feet and knees

squeezed tightly against each other.

Rest the top of your skull on the floor, if you wish,

Breathe deeply,

and with the palms of your hands

resting on the floor,

gently tilt your head backward.

and support yourself on your elbows.

Stay in this pose for a few moments.

Do you hear the sound of water flowing?

It washes over our hair,

our neck, our back. . . .

It's so cool! It feels good!

Now we are the river!

RIVER POSE

Sit on your mat,

legs stretched out in front of you

and back straight.

Breathe calmly,

then lean forward

and try to grab your toes or feet with your hands.

Rest your head on your legs, bending your knees a little if you wish.

Repeat this pose three times.

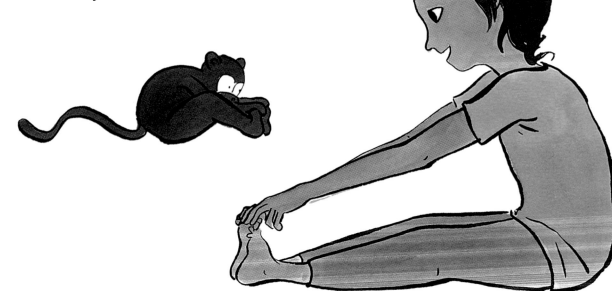

Should we take a little rest, Yazoo? When you're on a journey, sometimes you have to take a break!

This beautiful lotus flower is as comfortable as a couch!

We just sit here, close our eyes, breathe gently, and we don't think about anything.

We just feel good, that's all.

34

After this pose, go to page 44 and have someone read you "Under the Water."

HALF-LOTUS POSE

Sit in a cross-legged position,

back straight,

shoulders relaxed.

Put your right foot on your left thigh,

put your hands on your knees,

and close your eyes.

Take a deep breath in

and breathe out slowly.

Repeat twice on each side.

GUIDED MEDITATION for RELAXATION and CALM

IN THE SUN

Lie down on your back and close your eyes. Spread your arms and legs a little and turn the palms of your hands toward the sky. Breathe deeply. Your feet, legs, and belly relax. Your shoulders relax. Your neck, back, arms, and head relax. Your whole body becomes more and more relaxed.

Breathe calmly and let yourself be carried along by this story. It's a restful little journey. . . .

It's a lovely winter morning. You are sitting in your room on your bed. The window is slightly open. The sun is already beaming brightly in the sky. It's a huge yellow ball, shining in all its splendor. A beautiful day is beginning!

The air is a little chilly. The light breeze that blows into your room wakes up your skin. You breathe in the morning fragrances, the odors of toasting bread and hot chocolate! YOU FEEL GOOD.

Hey, the sun is in a good mood—it wants to play with you! It follows you, it tickles you, it wants to light up your whole body from the tips of your toes to the top of your head. Its rays are having a great time heating up your toes, legs, tummy, chest, arms, and the backs of your fingers. You feel the warm rays touching your nose, eyelids, forehead, and even your hair.

YOU ARE HAPPY that the sun is there with you, happy that it is sharing all its ENERGY with you. You feel its power and wisdom deeply.

And now, full of strength and life for this new day, it's your turn to shine. You are going to be radiant and full of light!

Now, very slowly, open your eyes. You can stretch your arms and legs. You can yawn if you feel like it and just lie there for a little while. Then, when you feel ready, get up.

IN THE GARDEN

Lie down on your back and close your eyes. Spread your arms and legs a little and turn the palms of your hands toward the sky. Breathe deeply. Your feet, legs, and belly relax. Your shoulders relax. Your neck, back, arms, and head relax. Your whole body becomes more and more relaxed.

Breathe calmly and let yourself be carried along by this story. It's a restful little journey. . . .

You are in front of a very pretty blue gate. You don't know what you're going to find on the other side, but you decide to go ahead and push it open. You discover A MAGNIFICENT GARDEN, full of flowers and big trees.

You take off your shoes and you feel the cool grass under your bare feet. You smile. Spring is finally here! You BREATHE, and you recognize the smell of freshly cut grass and then the odor of the damp earth after it rains.

Around you, the trees are covered with young leaves. You go up to one of the trees. It's one that you like a lot. Its roots poke up above the ground. Its bark is thick. It is very strong. It is probably more than a hundred years old! You touch its trunk and YOU FEEL PROTECTED by its presence. You, too, are both calm and strong.

This tree is a new friend. Listen to the song of the birds in its branches. They are calling you by your name, because they're happy you are there. You laugh!

Going further into the garden, you discover many, many flowers. There are purple ones, red ones, yellow ones . . .

You lie down on this many-colored carpet. HOW GOOD IT SMELLS! Above you, the sky is a beautiful blue. A gentle breeze caresses blows through your hair, and light wraps around you like a warm cocoon. This is so nice. YOU FEEL HAPPY TO BE HERE.

Now, very slowly, open your eyes. You can stretch your arms and legs. You can yawn if you feel like it and just lie there for a little while. Then, when you feel ready, get up.

IN THE SKY

Lie down on your back and close your eyes. Spread your arms and legs a little and turn the palms of your hands toward the sky. Breathe deeply. Your feet, legs, and belly relax. Your shoulders relax. Your neck, back, arms, and head relax. Your whole body becomes more and more relaxed.

Breathe calmly and let yourself be carried along by this story. It's a restful little journey. . . .

You live in a big city, in a very tall building. When you are out on the street, and you raise your head to look up at it, it seems like it pierces the clouds. Today is a Saturday, and you decide to go up to the terrace on the roof of your building. Hop! Hop! At the end you go up a few stairs, push open a little door, and you're there!

You take off your shoes. There's a lawn up here, just as green as the one in the park where you often play. You love coming up here for a rest whenever you have time. **YOU FEEL BIG AND STRONG.**

It's a magical spot that seems to float above the city. Beautiful white clouds cover the roofs of the houses, as well as the noise of the cars and the electric lights in the streets. How **SOFT** the clouds look! You have the urge to reach out and touch them. It would be like touching cotton candy! Look, there's a family of birds flying along among the clouds. You shout a loud "Good morning!" to them.

You walk over to the green wooden bench you're so familiar with, where you love to sit and read your favorite books. But who do you see there? Your best friend! She wanted to surprise you. **YOU ARE GLAD SHE'S THERE AND YOU LAUGH WITH HER.** The two of you together sit there in this wonderful nest high above the clouds and contemplate the horizon.

The blue sky starts to turn pink, and here's the moon coming up already, a big, white, radiant ball that will be shining brightly later on tonight. You and your friend will be going home now. **YOU FEEL CALM AND JOYFUL.**

Now, very slowly, open your eyes. You can stretch your arms and legs. You can yawn if you feel like it and just lie there for a little while. Then, when you feel ready, get up.

UNDER THE WATER

Lie down on your back and close your eyes. Spread your arms and legs a little and turn the palms of your hands toward the sky. Breathe deeply. Your feet, legs, and belly relax. Your shoulders relax. Your neck, back, arms, and head relax. Your whole body becomes more and more relaxed.

Breathe calmly and let yourself be carried along by this story. It's a restful little journey....

It's an afternoon in the summer, and you're walking along a very beautiful beach.

It's hot! You breathe and stretch while the sand tickles the soles of your feet. You are on vacation and have all your time to yourself. **WHAT HAPPINESS!**

How about plunging into the clear water to cool off? The sea is just over there, very blue, sparkling—it's waiting for you. Why not transform yourself into a silvery fish and join all those other little fish having fun in the waves? Jump in! A little splash and there you are underwater! **ALL IS CALM.**

You swim along slowly. You open your eyes wide. You feel the water slipping past your body. It gives you tiny tickles.

You are light, and you glide easily among the seaweed and the many-colored corals that decorate the sea floor. Some blue and yellow fish are racing each other, and some pretty clown fish are hiding among the anemones. An odd-looking crab is sidestepping along. A starfish is taking a nap partly covered up by a blanket of sand.

What a lot of interesting things to see at the bottom of the ocean. **YOU FEEL GOOD.** You're as agile as a dolphin. It's **MAGICAL** to move so easily through the water!

Oh! A column of bubbles. Surely they must belong to a fish who's chatting with his buddy. The bubbles are on their way up to the surface. You decide to follow those little round bubbles. The light gets brighter very quickly as you swim upward.

That's it! You've reached the surface! Your head is popping out of the water. And immediately you feel the sun and its GENTLE WARMTH. You swim back to the beach and you stretch out on the sand, right at the edge of the sea.

You have completed a marvelous journey to the land of the silver fish.

You made some great discoveries.

YOU ARE HAPPY AND YOU SMILE.

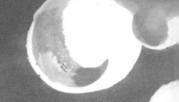

Now, very slowly, open your eyes. You can stretch your arms and legs. You can yawn if you feel like it and just lie there for a little while. Then, when you feel ready, get up.

NOTES FOR GROWN-UPS

The main purpose of this book is for children to learn and play. It's an easy introduction to the ancient practice of yoga, which for children can be a fascinating world to explore. Practicing yoga can help sensitize them to the world of animals and nature, while also helping them become aware of their own bodies.

how to do yoga with a child
This book offers two approaches to doing yoga with a child:

1   If children, alone or accompanied, want to do a whole session of yoga (roughly one hour), they can do all fourteen poses and then choose at least one of the four guided meditations to conclude the session.

2   For a shorter session of around fifteen minutes, pick just one of the chapters. Each one of the four chapters with its accompanying guided meditation can be treated as a complete session.

In this way, you can choose the session that best fits the schedule, interests, and needs of those who are going to participate.

When just starting out, children may need more guidance from you until they are more familiar with the poses. Practicing one-on-one alongside children can be very helpful, especially if a child is worried or stressed. It can be very nice to do yoga as a family, in small groups, or in a class.

Children will appreciate these special, playful moments spent with you and with Kika. Regular repetition of the poses in the order they are demonstrated in the book makes it possible to integrate them into daily life without any sense of competition or feeling the need to seek perfection. Ideally, children experience yoga as something to enjoy, not something they have to do.

Do not hesitate to let a child do a pose as many times as he or she wants to. If the child does a pose many times, you will quickly notice the beneficial physical and emotional effects of yoga.

Whether you are practicing or just leading and watching, encourage children to breathe in and out naturally and easily.

when to do yoga

This book is designed to make it easy for a child to go back and do Kika's poses whenever he or she feels like it, whether it is in the morning before school or childcare, before going to a party, on the weekend, during family time, or on vacation.

It is up to the child and you to have a sense of when the right time for practicing yoga might be and which poses might be the most helpful. For example, if the child needs support for concentrating in school, try the green chapter (pages 10–17), or try the blue chapter (pages 30–35) if the child needs to relax after a long day. If you incorporate the practice or a set of the poses into your routine consistently, you will notice the benefits of yoga for children.

Always follow up a ten-minute session by reading one of the guided meditations at the end of the book.

where to do yoga

The poses can be practiced at home, outdoors in a natural environment, at school, or at the gym. Children often enjoy creating their own imaginative setting and making up their own ritual in connection with the practice. Ideally, find a calm spot with plenty of room to do these yoga sessions and maybe even have soft music accompany them.

guided meditations

The guided meditations at the end of the book should ideally be read aloud by another person. They should be used at the end of each short session. They can also be used at any time during the day. For example, they can be read during a long plane or car trip in order to relieve the children's impatience.

Ideally, children should be lying down on the yoga mat or on a bed. You may want to accompany the reading with some peaceful music. Read in a soft voice and with a spacious rhythm. If it is a very sunny day, close the curtains of the room. If it is already dark outside, dim your inside lights a bit—they should not be too bright. Don't forget to turn off any noisy machines or devices, like cell phones, that may be around. If the temperature is a bit cool, offer the child a blanket and a pillow.

The calmer and more present you are when you are reading, the more children will experience the story as a moment of calm relaxation and a time conducive to dreaming. The important thing is the quality of this time you are spending with the children. Do not feel that you necessarily have to read the story exactly as written. Let yourself be carried along by the framework the story presents and do not hesitate to change it to better fit the character and content of the children's experience.